What Happens at a
Supermarket?

By Amy Hutchings

Reading Consultant: Susan Nations, M.Ed.,
author/literacy coach/consultant in literacy development

WEEKLY READER®
PUBLISHING

For a complete list of Where People Work titles,
please visit our web site at **www.garethstevens.com**.
For a free catalog describing Gareth Stevens Publishing's list of high-quality books,
call 1-800-542-2595 (USA) or 1-800-387-3178 (Canada). Our fax: 877-542-2596

Library of Congress Cataloging-in-Publication Data

Hutchings, Amy.
     What happens at a supermarket? / by Amy Hutchings.
        p. cm. — (Where people work)
     Includes bibliographical references and index.
     ISBN-10: 1-4339-0069-6   ISBN-13: 978-1-4339-0069-3 (lib. bdg.)
     ISBN-10: 1-4339-0133-1   ISBN-13: 978-1-4339-0133-1 (softcover)
     1. Supermarkets—Juvenile literature. I. Title.
  HF5469.H88   2009
  381'.456413-dc22

                                      2008032229

This edition first published in 2009 by
Weekly Reader® Books
An Imprint of Gareth Stevens Publishing
1 Reader's Digest Road
Pleasantville, NY 10570-7000 USA

Executive Managing Editor: Lisa M. Herrington
Creative Director: Lisa Donovan
Designers: Michelle Castro, Alexandria Davis
Photographer: Richard Hutchings
Publisher: Keith Garton

Special thanks to the Stop & Shop Supermarket Company and to store managers Bob Silver
and Gary DaVita.

Printed in the United States of America

1 2 3 4 5 6 7 8 9 10 09 08

Hi, Kids!

I'm Buddy, your Weekly Reader® pal. Have you ever been to a supermarket? I'm here to show and tell what happens at a supermarket. So, come on. Turn the page and read along!

Boldface words appear in the glossary.

3

Welcome to the **supermarket**! A supermarket is a store where people buy food and other items.

Big trucks bring food to the supermarket. Workers unload boxes of food from the trucks.

Produce workers put out fresh fruits and vegetables. Yum! Look at all the bright yellow bananas.

Some workers stock the shelves with food. They make sure that shoppers can find what they need.

The supermarket also has a bakery. The **baker** makes fresh bread and rolls. She frosts a birthday cake.

baker

13

In the **deli**, busy workers slice fresh meat and cheese for sandwiches. They are very careful with the slicing machines.

deli

Behind the scenes, a worker puts out new cartons of milk. He makes sure that milk and other **dairy** foods are fresh.

When shoppers are done, they go to the checkout line. They pay the **cashier** for their groceries.

cashier

19

A bagger puts groceries into cloth bags. The bags can be used for the next visit to the supermarket.

bagger

🐻 Glossary

baker: a person who makes baked goods, such as bread, rolls, cookies, and cakes

cashier: a person who takes in and pays out money in a store

dairy: milk and milk products, such as cheese, butter, and yogurt

deli: a place where ready-to-eat foods such as meat, cheese, and prepared salads are sold

produce: fresh fruits and vegetables

supermarket: a store where people buy groceries

For More Information

Books

Grocery Store. Field Trip (series). Angela Leeper (Heinemann, 2004)

My Food Pyramid. (DK Publishing, 2007)

Supermarket. Kathleen Krull (Holiday House, 2001)

Web Site

PBS Kids: Supermarket Adventure
www.pbskids.org/arthur/games/supermarket
Go grocery shopping with this exciting supermarket game!

# Index

About the Author

Amy Hutchings was part of the original production staff of *Sesame Street* for the first ten years of the show's history. She then went on to work with her husband, Richard, producing thousands of photographs for children's publishers. She has written several books, including *Firehouse Dog* and *Picking Apples and Pumpkins*. She lives in Rhinebeck, New York, along with many deer, squirrels, and wild turkeys.